ESSENTIAL ELEMENTS

PIANO THEORY

T0071722

ISBN 978-1-4803-6317-5

HAL•LEONARD®

7777 W. BLUEMOUND RD. P.O. BOX 13819 MILWAUKEE, WI 53213

Visit Hal Leonard Online at
www.halleonard.com

Contact us:
Hal Leonard
7777 West Bluemound Road
Milwaukee, WI 53213
Email: info@halleonard.com

In Europe, contact:
Hal Leonard Europe Limited
42 Wigmore Street
Marylebone, London, W1U 2RN
Email: info@halleonardeurope.com

In Australia, contact:
Hal Leonard Australia Pty. Ltd.
4 Lentara Court
Cheltenham, Victoria, 3192 Australia
Email: info@halleonard.com.au

To the Student

I wrote these books with you in mind. As a young student I often wondered how completing theory work-books would make me a better musician. The theory work often seemed separate from the music I was play-ing. My goal in *Essential Elements Piano Theory* is to provide you with the tools you will need to compose, improvise, play classical and popular music, or to better understand any other musical pursuit you might en-joy. In each "Musical Mastery" section of this book you will experience creative applications of the theory you have learned. The "Ear Training" pages will be completed with your teacher at the lesson. In this series you will begin to learn the building blocks of music, which make it possible for you to have fun at the piano. A practical understanding of theory enables you to see what is possible in music. I wish you all the best on your journey as you learn the language of music!

Sincerely,
Mona Rejino

To the Teacher

I believe that knowledge of theory is most beneficial when a concept is followed directly by a musical application. In *Essential Elements Piano Theory*, learning theory becomes far more than completing worksheets. Students have the opportunity to see why learning a particular concept can help them become a better pianist right away. They can also see how the knowledge of musical patterns and chord progressions will enable them to be creative in their own musical pursuits: composing, arrang-ing, improvising, playing classical and popular music, accompanying, or any other.

A free download of the *Teacher's Answer Key* is available at www.halleonard.com/eeptheory5answer.

Acknowledgements

I would like to thank Hal Leonard Corporation for providing me the opportunity to put these theoret-ical thoughts down on paper and share them with others. I owe a debt of gratitude to Jennifer Linn, who has helped with this project every step of the way. These books would not have been possible without the support of my family: To my husband, Richard, for his wisdom and amazing ability to solve dilemmas; to my children, Maggie and Adam, for helping me think outside the box.

TABLE OF CONTENTS

UNIT 1 **Review** **4**
Notes • Rests • Counting • Ledger Line Notes • Intervals
Major Scales • Key Signatures • Tonic

UNIT 2 **Time Signatures and Rhythm** **7**
3/8 • 6/8 • Triplet • Syncopation

UNIT 3 **Primary Triads in Major Keys** **12**
Tonic • Subdominant • Dominant

UNIT 4 **Triads and Inversions** **14**
Root Position • 1st Inversion • 2nd Inversion

MUSICAL MASTERY **17**
Ear Training • Analysis • Reading Mastery

UNIT 5 **Minor Key Signatures** **20**
Relative Minor Keys (C/a, G/e, D/b, F/d, and B♭/g)

UNIT 6 **Relative Minor Scales** **22**
a, e, b, d, and g minor

UNIT 7 **Forms of Minor Scales** **24**
Natural • Harmonic • Melodic

UNIT 8 **Major and Minor Triads** **27**
Major 3rds • Minor 3rds • Perfect 5ths
Identifying and Naming Major and Minor Triads

UNIT 9 **Primary Triads in Minor Keys** **29**
Tonic • Subdominant • Dominant

MUSICAL MASTERY **31**
Ear Training • Match Game • Key Signature Discoveries

UNIT 10 **Musical Signs and Terms** **35**
Tempo • Articulation • Mood • Symbols

UNIT 11 **Review** **38**
Terms and Symbols • Time Signatures • Rhythms • Syncopation
Relative Major and Minor Key Signatures • Primary Triads
Root Position, 1st Inversion and 2nd Inversion Triads
Minor Scales • Identifying Triads in a Key

MUSICAL MASTERY **42**
Ear Training • Analysis • Reading Mastery

THEORY MASTERY **45**
Review Test • Ear Training

REVIEW

1. Draw one note in each box to solve the music math equations. *The first one is done for you.*

2. Each measure below is incomplete. Draw one **note** in each box to complete the measure.

3. Each measure below is incomplete. Draw one **rest** in each box to complete the measure.

4. Add the missing bar lines to the rhythm. Write the counts below each measure.

5. Name the following ledger line notes.

6. Name these intervals.

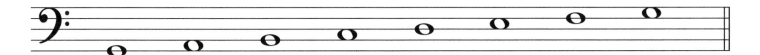

7. On each staff below, add the sharps or flats needed to form these Major scales. Mark the half steps with a curved line. Use the Major scale pattern: 1 W 2 W 3 H 4 W 5 W 6 W 7 H 8

G Major

F Major

D Major

C Major

B♭ Major

5. Each row contains one scale, key signature or tonic (keynote) that does not belong in the given key. Place an "X" through the one that doesn't belong.

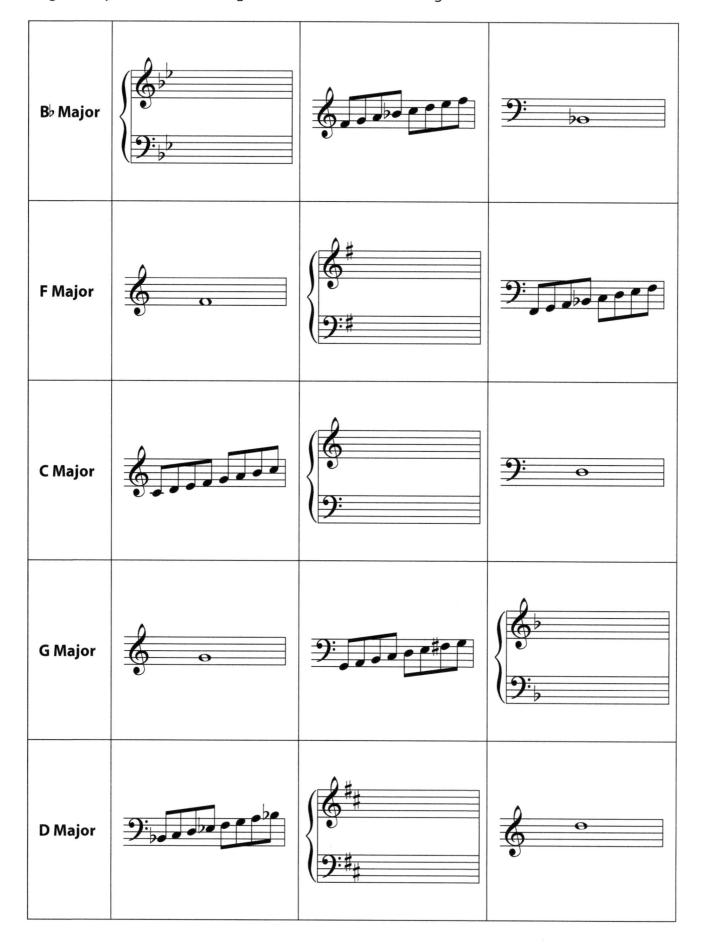

Time Signatures and Rhythm

A **TIME SIGNATURE** tells two things:

Top number = How many beats are in each measure

Bottom number = What kind of note gets one beat

3 = 3 beats in a measure
8 = eighth note () gets one beat

In **3/8** time: ♪ = 1 beat   ♩ = 2 beats   ♩. = 3 beats

1. Clap and count this rhythm.

$\frac{3}{8}$

1   2   3 | 1   2   3 | 1   2   3 | 1   2   3

2. Write the counts below each measure, then clap and count the rhythm.

$\frac{3}{8}$

3. Add bar lines where needed. Write the counts below each measure. Choose one key on the piano and play the rhythm while counting aloud.

$\frac{3}{8}$

⁶⁄₈ TIME SIGNATURE

6 = 6 beats in a measure

8 = eighth note (♪) gets one beat

NOTES	RESTS	NUMBER OF BEATS
♪	୨	1
♩	𝄽	2
♩.	𝄾.	3
♩. (half dotted)	−	6

4. Write the number of beats each note or rest receives in ⁶⁄₈ time.

♪ = ___   ♩ = ___   ♩. = ___   𝅗𝅥. = ___   𝄽 = ___   𝄾. = ___   ୨ = ___

5. Clap and count this rhythm.

1 2 3 4 5 6   1 2 3 4 5 6   1 2 3 4 5 6   1 2 3 4 5 6

6. Write the counts below each measure, then clap and count the rhythm.

7. Add bar lines where needed. Write the counts below each measure. Choose one key on the piano and play the rhythm while counting aloud.

In faster tempos, $\frac{6}{8}$ can be counted with 2 beats per measure, "in 2."

8. Write the counts below each measure in a fast $\frac{6}{8}$. Choose one key on the piano and play the rhythm "in 2," while counting aloud. *The first measure is done for you.*

9. Some measures below have the wrong number of counts. Draw an "X" through any measures that are incorrect. *Notice the time signature.*

The **EIGHTH NOTE TRIPLET** = 1 beat of sound

The word **triplet** means three.

An eighth note triplet is equal to one quarter note in $\frac{2}{4}$, $\frac{3}{4}$, or $\frac{4}{4}$ time.

10. Clap and count this rhythm, keeping a steady beat.

11. Write the counts below each measure, then clap and count each rhythm.

12. Draw an eighth note triplet in each box. Choose one key on the piano and play the rhythm.

SYNCOPATION occurs in rhythm when emphasis is placed on a weak beat instead of a strong beat. When a long note is played on the weak part of a beat, the rhythm is **syncopated**.

13. Write the counts below each measure. Circle each long note that comes on a weak beat. Choose one key on the piano and play each rhythm.

Primary Triads in Major Keys

Triads built on the 1st, 4th and 5th notes of a Major scale are called **PRIMARY TRIADS**.

Primary Triads are labeled with Roman numerals.

I = Tonic   **IV = Subdominant**   **V = Dominant**

Primary Triads in C Major are:

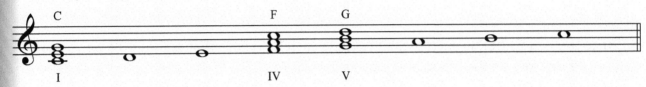

The triad is named by its root (lowest note). In Major keys, primary triads are Major triads.

1. Draw the primary triads on the 1st, 4th and 5th note of each scale. Label the primary triads in two ways: Roman numerals below, and letter names above. *Notice the key signature when identifying letter names.*

C Major

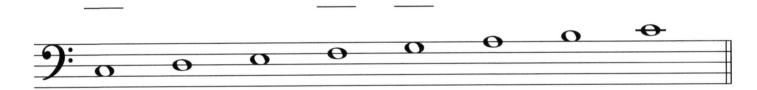

F Major

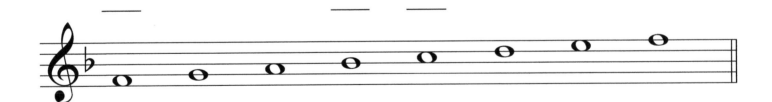

G Major

D Major

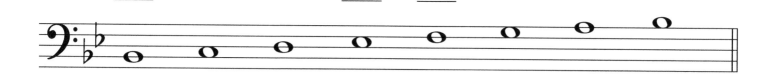

B♭ Major

2. Draw the chords (triads) indicated in each Major key below. Use whole notes. Play each example on the piano.

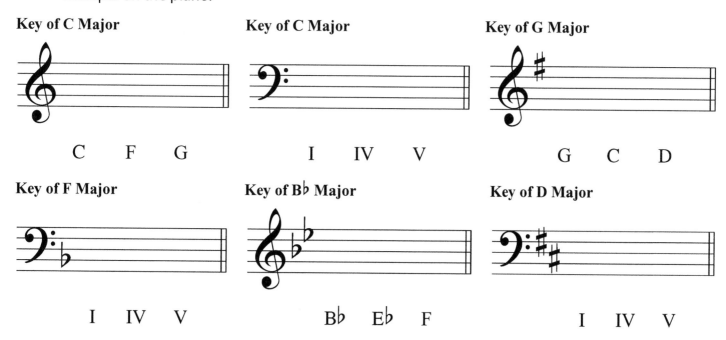

Key of C Major

C   F   G

Key of C Major

I   IV   V

Key of G Major

G   C   D

Key of F Major

I   IV   V

Key of B♭ Major

B♭   E♭   F

Key of D Major

I   IV   V

Triads and Inversions

TRIADS have three positions: **Root Position, 1st Inversion** and **2nd Inversion.**

Root Position Triads consist of intervals of a 3rd.

The notes of a root position triad may be rearranged to form inversions. The letter names stay the same.

Root Position: root is lowest note

1st Inversion: 3rd is lowest note

2nd Inversion: 5th is lowest note

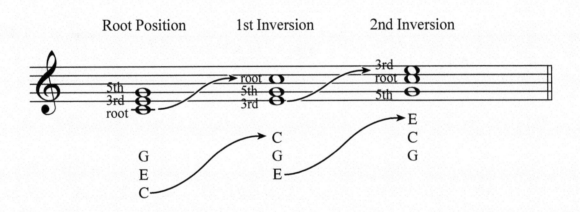

Triads in 1st inversion and 2nd inversion consist of an interval of a 3rd and an interval of a 4th. The top note of the 4th is the root.

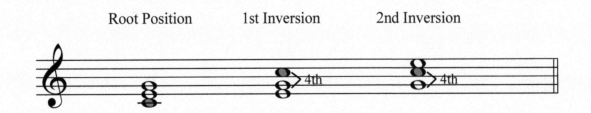

1. Draw the inversions of these triads. Add accidentals where needed.

Root Position	1st Inversion	2nd Inversion

D minor

G Major

F minor

A Major

E minor

Bb Major

2. Fill in the root in these 1st inversion triads. *The first one is done for you.*

3. Fill in the root in these 2nd inversion triads. *The first one is done for you.*

4. Name the root in each triad. *The first one is done for you.*

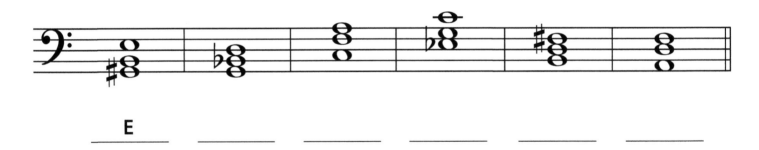

      E   ___   ___   ___   ___   ___

___   ___   ___   ___   ___   ___

MUSICAL MASTERY

Ear Training

1. You will hear one rhythm from each pair. Circle the rhythm you hear.

2. You will hear intervals of a 2nd, 3rd, 5th or 7th played in broken and blocked form. Name the correct interval in each blank.

    1. _____   2. _____   3. _____   4. _____   5. _____   6. _____

3. You will hear four measures of melodic dictation. Fill in the blank measures with the notes and rhythms you hear.

4. One chord is missing from each group below. Listen for the missing blocked root position chord. Write I, IV or V in each box.

    a. I   IV   V   b. I   IV   I

    c. I   IV   V   d. I   V   IV

    e.   V   IV   I   f. I   IV   I

Analysis

Follow the directions under each musical excerpt.

Allegretto by Gurlitt

1. What kind of note gets one count? _____

2. Name the key signature. _____

3. Write the counts under each note and rest.

4. Play the excerpt.

Etude, Op. 823 No. 15 by Czerny

1. Name the key signature. _____

2. Block the circled triad. Is it in root position, 1st inversion or 2nd inversion? _____

3. Write the counts under each note, counting in a slow $\frac{6}{8}$ tempo.

4. Play the excerpt.

Ecossaise by Beethoven

1. Name the key signature. _____

2. Write the counts under each note and rest.

3. Circle the syncopated rhythms.

4. Play the excerpt.

Reading Mastery

The following piece uses root position primary triads in the key of C Major as the basis for its harmony.

1. Play "Cool Triplets Rule."

Cool Triplets Rule

Mona Rejino

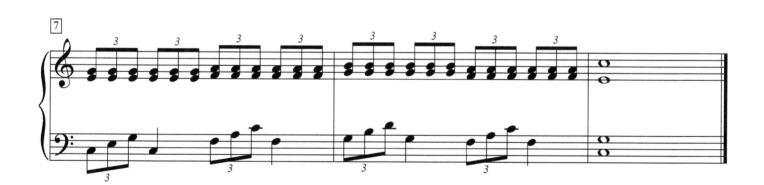

UNIT 5

Minor Key Signatures

Every Major key has a **RELATIVE MINOR KEY** which uses the same key signature. To find the relative minor key, count down three half steps from the tonic of the Major key.

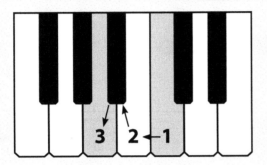

C Major and A minor share the same key signature: *no sharps and no flats*

1. Find the relative minor key for the Major keys below. On each keyboard, count down three half steps from the shaded key. Fill in the blank with the correct letter.

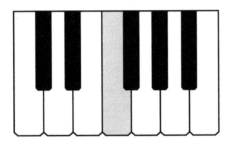

F Major and _____ minor share the same key signature: *one flat, B♭*

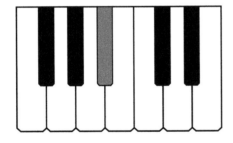

B♭ Major and _____ minor share the same key signature: *two flats, B♭ and E♭*

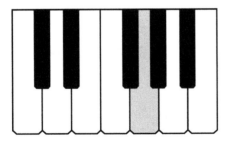

G Major and _____ minor share the same key signature: *one sharp, F#*

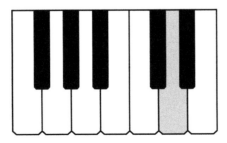

D Major and _____ minor share the same key signature: *two sharps, F# and C#*

2. Name the Major and relative minor keys for each key signature.

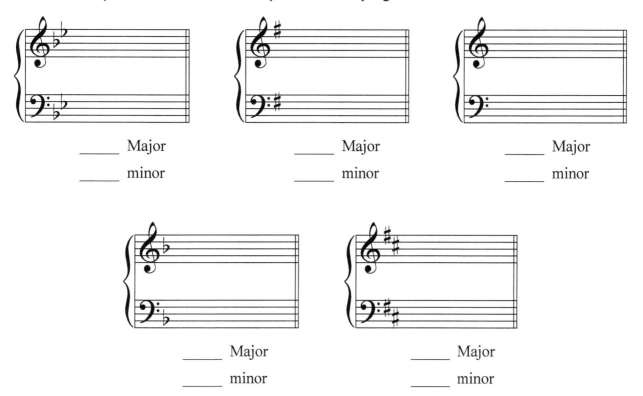

_____ Major   _____ Major   _____ Major

_____ minor   _____ minor   _____ minor

_____ Major   _____ Major

_____ minor   _____ minor

3. Draw the minor key signature named below each measure in both clefs, then draw the tonic (keynote.) *The first one is done for you.*

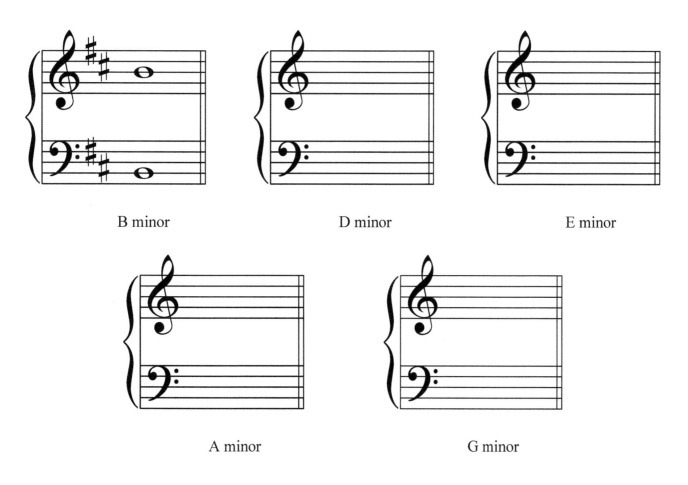

B minor   D minor   E minor

A minor   G minor

Relative Minor Scales

Every Major scale has a **RELATIVE MINOR SCALE** which uses the same key signature. The relative minor scale begins on the sixth note (degree) of the Major scale.

C Major Scale

A Natural Minor Scale

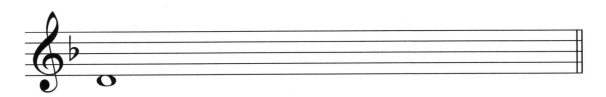

1. Draw the notes of the D natural minor scale. It is the relative minor scale of F Major.

F Major Scale

D Natural Minor Scale

2. Draw the notes of the A natural minor scale. It is the relative minor scale of C Major.

C Major Scale

A Natural Minor Scale

3. Draw the notes of the E natural minor scale. It is the relative minor scale of G Major.

G Major Scale

E Natural Minor Scale

4. Draw the notes of the G natural minor scale. It is the relative minor scale of B♭ Major.

B♭ Major Scale

G Natural Minor Scale

5. Draw the notes of the B natural minor scale. It is the relative minor scale of D Major.

D Major Scale

B Natural Minor Scale

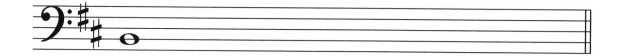

Forms of Minor Scales

Each Major scale has only one form. Each minor scale has three forms: **Natural**, **Harmonic** and **Melodic**.

Natural Minor Scale

The notes follow the key signature with no changes.

Harmonic Minor Scale

The seventh note is raised a half step ascending and descending.

Melodic Minor Scale

The sixth and seventh notes are raised a half step ascending, then are lowered descending. The melodic minor scale descending is the same as the natural minor scale.

1. Below each natural minor scale, draw the harmonic and melodic forms of that minor scale. Use accidentals where needed. *Notice the key signature.*

E Natural Minor

E Harmonic Minor

E Melodic Minor

D Natural Minor

D Harmonic Minor

D Melodic Minor

B Natural Minor

B Harmonic Minor

B Melodic Minor

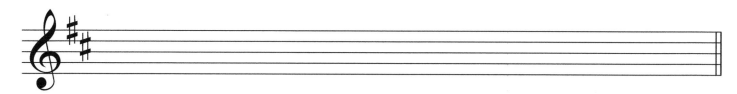

G Natural Minor

G Harmonic Minor

G Melodic Minor

Major and Minor Triads

A **MAJOR 3RD** is made up of 4 half steps.

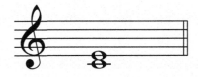

A **MINOR 3RD** is made up of 3 half steps.

A **MAJOR TRIAD** has a Major 3rd on the bottom and a minor 3rd on top.

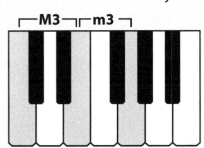

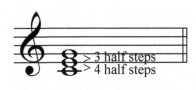

> 3 half steps
> 4 half steps

A **MINOR TRIAD** has a minor 3rd on the bottom and a Major 3rd on top.

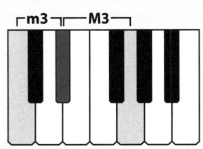

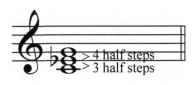

> 4 half steps
> 3 half steps

A **PERFECT 5TH** consists of 7 half steps. The interval between the root and 5th of a Major or minor triad forms a Perfect 5th.

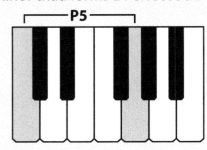

> 7 half steps

1. In the box below each keyboard, write the letter name of the triad. Tell whether it is Major or minor. *The first one is done for you.*

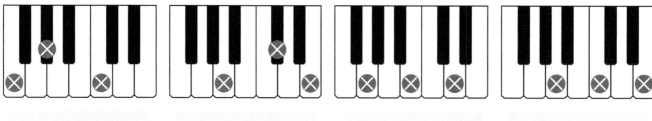

F minor

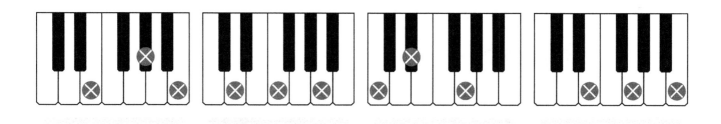

2. Write the letter name of the root in the box above each triad. If the triad is minor, add a small m after the root letter name. *The first two are done for you.*

Fm   D

Primary Triads in Minor Keys

Triads built on the 1st, 4th and 5th notes of a minor scale are called **PRIMARY TRIADS**.

Primary Triads are labeled with Roman numerals.

i = Tonic   **iv = Subdominant**   **V = Dominant**

Primary Triads in A minor are:

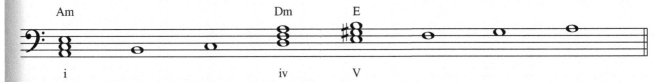

In minor keys, the i and iv chords are minor. The V chord is Major. The 3rd of the V chord is raised a half step to form a Major triad.

1. Draw the primary triads on the 1st, 4th and 5th note of each scale. Label the primary triads in two ways: Roman numerals below, and letter names above. *Notice the key signature when identifying letter names. Remember to raise the 3rd of each V chord a half step.*

A minor

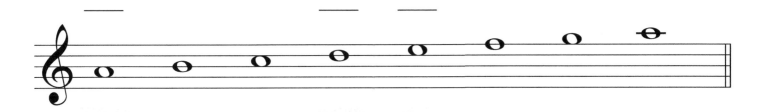

E minor

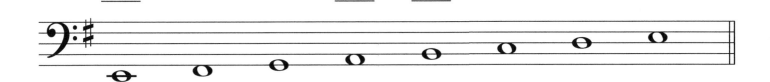

B minor

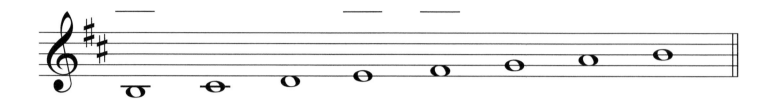

D minor

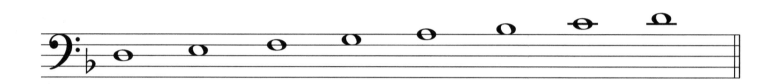

G minor

2. Draw the chords (triads) indicated in each minor key below. Use whole notes. Play each example on the piano.

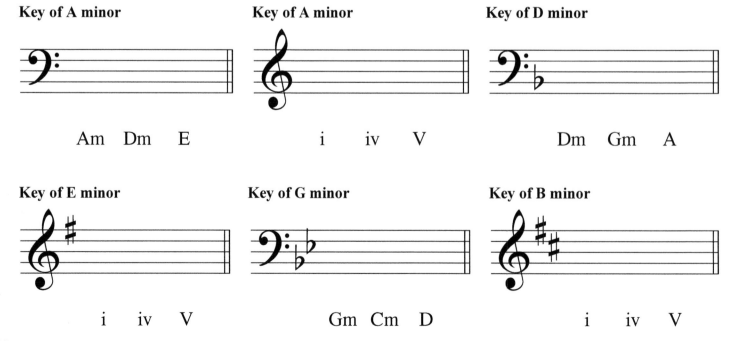

Key of A minor

Am   Dm   E

Key of A minor

i   iv   V

Key of D minor

Dm   Gm   A

Key of E minor

i   iv   V

Key of G minor

Gm   Cm   D

Key of B minor

i   iv   V

MUSICAL MASTERY

Ear Training

1. You will hear four measures of rhythmic dictation. Fill in the blank measures with the rhythm you hear.

2. The first melody in each pair is Major. The second melody in each pair is minor. Circle the one you hear.

1.

2.

3.

3. You will hear six scales. Each will ascend and descend. Identify each scale as either Major (**Maj.**) or natural minor (**nat. min.**).

1. _____ 2. _____ 3. _____ 4. _____ 5. _____ 6. _____

The Match Game

1. Match each term or symbol with its description by writing the correct number in the blank.

1. I   _____ 5th is lowest note

2. 1st inversion triad   _____ dominant

3. Major 3rd   _____ 3rd is lowest note

4. V   _____ W W H W W W H

5. Perfect 5th   _____ subdominant

6. IV   _____ tonic

7. 2nd inversion triad   _____ harmonic minor scale

8. Major scale   _____ made up of 4 half steps

9. relative keys   _____ made up of 3 half steps

10. 7th note is raised a half step   _____ root is lowest note

11. minor 3rd   _____ made up of 7 half steps

12. forms of minor scales   _____ emphasis on a weak beat

13. root position triad   _____ natural, harmonic and melodic

14. syncopation   _____ share the same key signature

Key Signature Discoveries

1. Name the tonic (I) and dominant (V) notes for these Major scales. *The first one is done for you.*

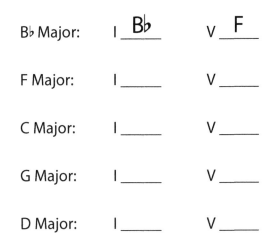

B♭ Major: I __B♭__   V __F__

F Major: I _____   V _____

C Major: I _____   V _____

G Major: I _____   V _____

D Major: I _____   V _____

2. In each blank write the letter name of the interval that is a Perfect 5th (7 half steps) up or down from **C**. Use capital letters.

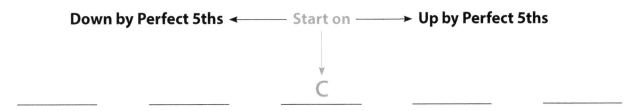

Down by Perfect 5ths ⟵ — Start on — ⟶ **Up by Perfect 5ths**

C

_____   _____   _____   _____   _____

3. Play the following Major 5-finger patterns.

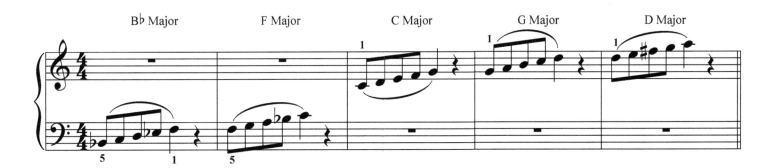

4. Name the tonic (i) and dominant (V) notes for these minor scales. *The first one is done for you.*

g minor: i _g_   V _d_

d minor: i _____   V _____

a minor: i _____   V _____

e minor: i _____   V _____

b minor: i _____   V _____

5. In each blank write the letter name of the interval that is a Perfect 5th (7 half steps) up or down from **a**. Use lower case letters.

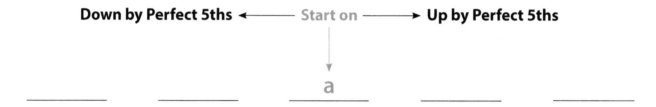

Down by Perfect 5ths ⟵ Start on ⟶ **Up by Perfect 5ths**

a

_____   _____   _____   _____   _____

6. Play the following minor 5-finger patterns.

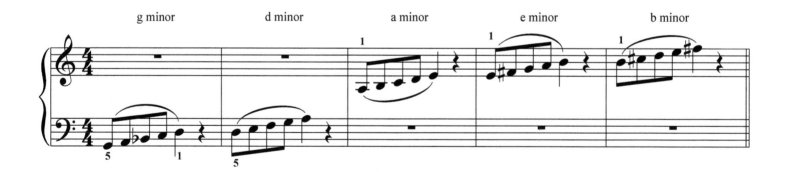

Musical Signs and Terms

An asterisk (*) indicates words that are new to this book.

TEMPO marks tell what speed to play the music.

Italian Name	Meaning
largo	slow and broad, slower than *adagio*
andantino	slightly faster than *andante*
allegretto	moderately fast, slightly slower than *allegro*
vivace	lively, quick
presto	very fast
accelerando (accel.)	becoming gradually faster
rallentando*	slowing the tempo
piu mosso*	more motion; quicker
meno mosso*	less motion; slower
con brio*	with spirit
con moto*	with motion

1. In each blank write the Italian name for the following tempo marks.

slightly faster than *andante* _____

lively, quick _____   slowing the tempo _____

with spirit _____   very fast _____

slow and broad, slower than *adagio* _____

becoming gradually faster _____

with motion _____   more motion; quicker _____

moderately fast, slightly slower than *allegro* _____

less motion; slower _____

ARTICULATION signs tell how to play and release the keys.

Name	Sign (Symbol)	Meaning
sforzando	*sfz* or *sf*	sudden, strong accent

The following terms help to describe the **mood** or **style** of the music.

Italian Name	Meaning
dolce	sweetly
grazioso	gracefully
maestoso	majestic; stately
poco	little
molto	very
allargando*	growing broader and slower
espressivo*	expressively
poco a poco*	little by little
sempre*	always
subito*	suddenly

2. In the blanks write the definition for each term.

poco _____   allargando _____

sempre _____   grazioso _____

sforzando _____   molto _____

dolce _____   espressivo _____

subito _____   maestoso _____

poco a poco _____

Other Musical Symbols

 Dal segno* (D.S.) means to return to the sign 𝄋.

D.S. al Fine* means to return to the sign 𝄋 and play to *fine* (the end).

 Coda sign* means to skip to the *Coda* (ending section).

D.C. al Coda* means to return to the beginning and play to ⊕, then skip to the *Coda* (ending section).

D.S. al Coda* means to return to the 𝄋 and play to ⊕, then skip to the *Coda* (ending section).

3. Clap the first four measures of the rhythm below. Return to the beginning and clap to ⊕, then skip to the *Coda*.

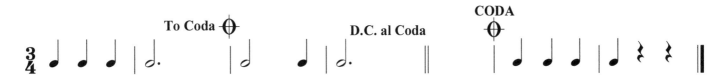

4. Clap the first six measures of the rhythm below. Return to the 𝄋 and clap to ⊕, then skip to the *Coda*.

REVIEW

1. Match each term with its definition by writing the correct letter in the blank.

_____ sempre   a. growing broader and slower

_____ allargando   b. suddenly

_____ meno mosso   c. always

_____ coda   d. return to 𝄋, play to 𝄌, skip to *Coda*

_____ molto   e. with spirit

_____ con brio   f. less motion; slower

_____ D.S. al Coda   g. very

_____ poco a poco   h. with motion

_____ rallentando   i. ending section

_____ subito   j. more motion; quicker

_____ accelerando   k. little by little

_____ piu mosso   l. expressively

_____ D.C. al Coda   m. slowing the tempo

_____ con moto   n. becoming gradually faster

_____ espressivo   o. return to beginning, play to 𝄌, skip to *Coda*

2. Fill in the blanks with the correct number or note value for each time signature.

3 = _____ beats per measure   3 = _____ beats per measure   6 = _____ beats per measure

4 = _____ gets one beat   8 = _____ gets one beat   8 = _____ gets one beat

3. Write the correct time signature in the boxes for each rhythm below.
   Choose from $\frac{2}{4}$ $\frac{3}{4}$ $\frac{4}{4}$ $\frac{3}{8}$ $\frac{6}{8}$.

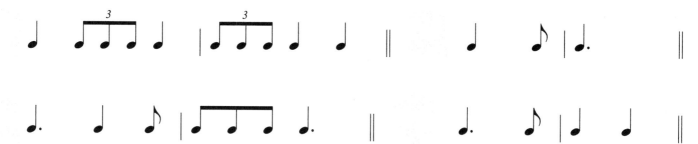

4. Write the counts below each measure. *Notice the time signature.*

5. Circle the measures below that contain syncopated rhythms.

6. Name the relative minor key for each Major key signature. *Count down three half steps from the tonic of the Major key.*

F Major   D Major   C Major   B♭ Major   G Major

____ minor   ____ minor   ____ minor   ____ minor   ____ minor

7. Label the primary triads with Roman numerals in each box. Choose from **I**, **i**, **IV**, **iv**, and **V**. Fill in the blank with the correct Major or minor key signature for each example.

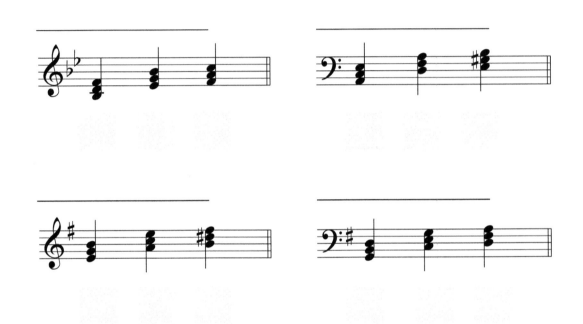

8. Draw the first inversion and second inversion triads from the root position triads given.

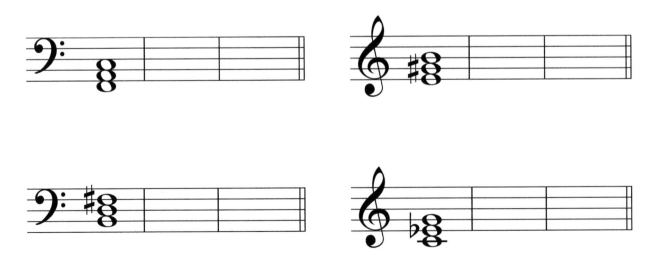

40

9. Mark each statement as either true or false.

_____ a. A Major triad is made up a Major 3rd and a minor 3rd.

_____ b. In a natural minor scale, the seventh scale degree is raised a half step.

_____ c. The interval between the root and fifth of a Major or minor triad forms a Perfect 5th.

_____ d. The melodic minor scale descending is the same as the natural minor scale.

_____ e. A Perfect 5th consists of eight half steps.

10. Add accidentals to complete the following scales.

G Harmonic Minor

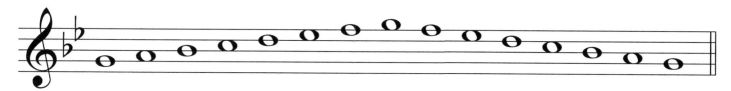

A Melodic Minor

11. Circle the correct Roman numeral to identify each triad in that key signature.

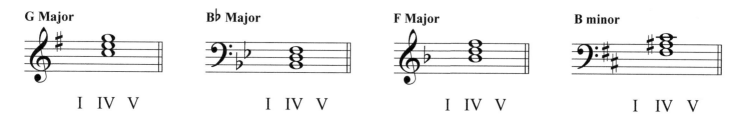

G Major   B♭ Major   F Major   B minor

I IV V   I IV V   I IV V   I IV V

MUSICAL MASTERY

Ear Training

1. You will hear four measures of rhythmic dictation. Fill in the blank measures with the rhythm you hear.

2. You will hear six intervals. Circle the interval you hear from each pair.

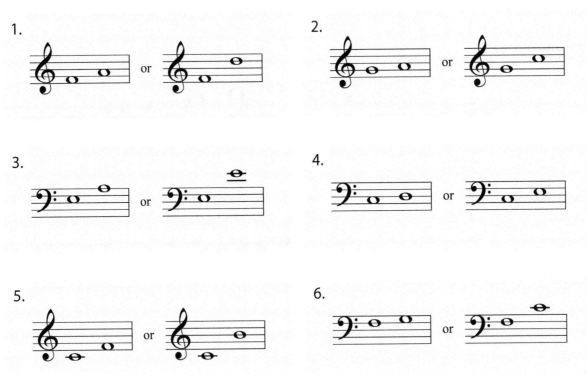

3. You will hear four measures of melodic dictation. Fill in the blank measures with the notes and rhythms you hear.

Analysis

Study this excerpt from "Wild Rider," then answer the questions about it.

Wild Rider

Robert Schumann
(1810–1856)

1. The circled triad in measure 1 is a Tonic triad. What is the key signature of this piece?

   _____

2. Is the circled triad in measure 3 Major or minor? _____

3. Is the circled triad in measure 6 in root position, first inversion or second inversion?

   _____

4. What does *sf* mean? _____

5. The note in the incomplete measure before measure 1 is called an _____ .

6. What is the time signature of this piece? _____

7. What kind of note gets one beat in this time signature? _____

8. Is the circled interval in measure 5 a Major 3rd or a minor 3rd? _____

9. How many G sharps are in measure 7? _____

Reading Mastery

"Boogie to the Blues" is based on a 12-bar blues harmonic pattern. In the bass clef, the first three notes in measures 1, 3, 5, 7, 9, 10 and 11 outline a primary triad in the key of C Major. The chords in the treble clef are in root position, first inversion and second inversion. Measure 12 includes syncopation.

1. Play "Boogie to the Blues."

Boogie to the Blues

Mona Rejino

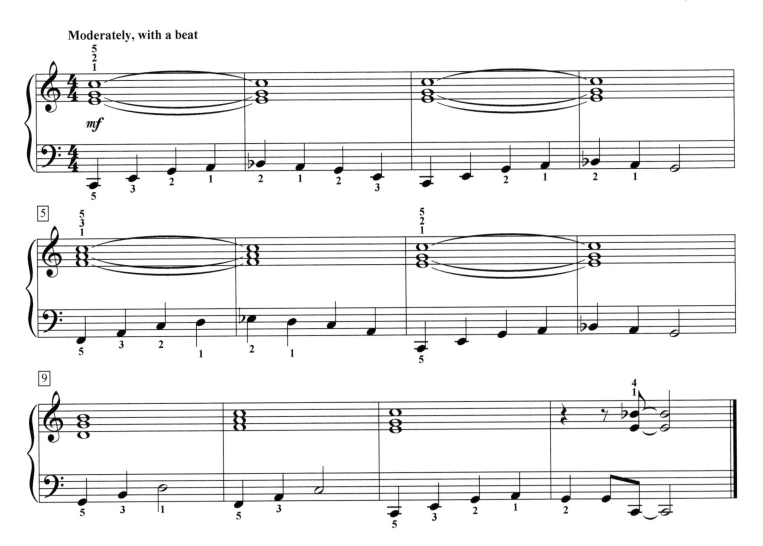

THEORY MASTERY

Review Test

1. Draw the bar lines where they are needed.

2. In each box draw one note to complete the measure.

3. Fill in the blanks.

    a. A _____ triad has a Major 3rd on the bottom and a minor 3rd on top.

    b. A _____ triad has a minor 3rd on the bottom and a Major 3rd on top.

4. Label each root position triad as Major or minor.

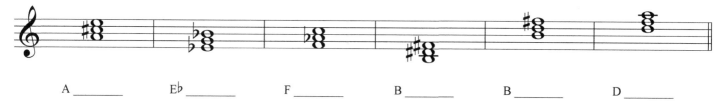

   A _____   Eb _____   F _____   B _____   B _____   D _____

5. Draw these triads in root position, first inversion and second inversion. Add accidentals as needed.

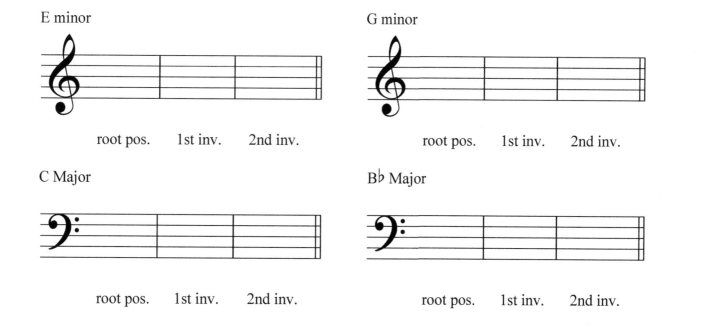

45

6. Name these Major and relative minor key signatures. In the first blank, name the Major key. In the second blank, name the minor key.

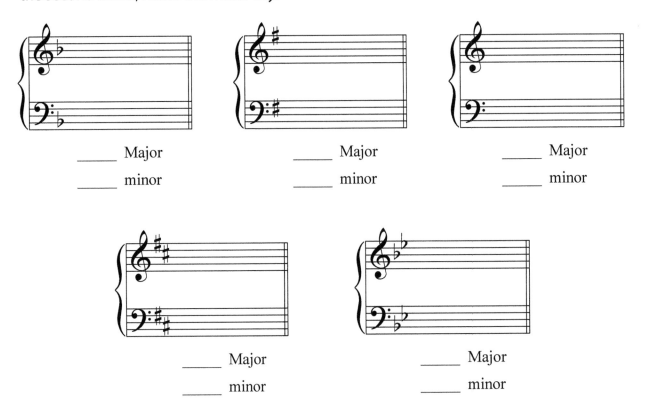

_____ Major

_____ minor

_____ Major

_____ minor

_____ Major

_____ minor

_____ Major

_____ minor

_____ Major

_____ minor

7. Add the correct accidentals to form these scales.

D Natural Minor

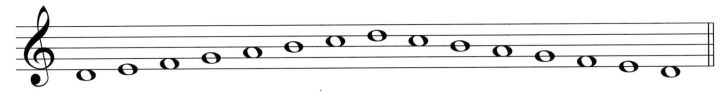

B Harmonic Minor

E Melodic Minor

8. Draw the corresponding root position triads in each key.

D minor	D Major	G minor	E minor	C Major

i   V   iv   V   IV

9. Fill in the blanks with the correct answer.

a. How many half steps are in a Perfect 5th? _____

b. Triads built on the 1st, 4th and 5th notes of a scale are called _____ triads.

c. The _____ minor scale uses the key signature of the relative Major scale with no changes.

d. In a Major key, the Roman numeral for a subdominant chord is _____.

e. Root position triads consist of intervals of a _____.

f. Triads in 1st inversion and 2nd inversion consist of an interval of a 3rd and an interval of a _____.

g. The _____ minor scale is different ascending and descending.

h. How many half steps are there between a Major key and its relative minor?

_____

i. The relative minor scale begins on the _____ note (degree) of its relative major scale.

j. In a harmonic minor scale, the _____ scale degree of a natural minor scale is raised a half step.

Ear Training

1. You will hear one rhythm from each pair. Circle the rhythm you hear.

1.
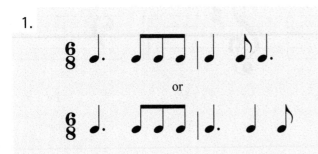

2.
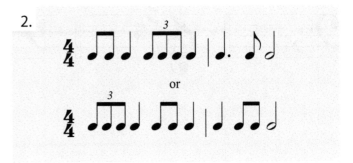

2. You will hear intervals of a 2nd, 3rd, 5th or 7th played in broken and blocked form. Name the correct interval in each blank

1. _____ 2. _____ 3. _____ 4. _____ 5. _____ 6. _____

3. You will hear four measures of melodic dictation. Fill in the blank measures with the notes and rhythms you hear.

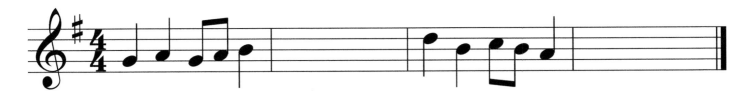

4. You will hear six scales ascending and descending. Identify each scale as Major **(Maj.)** or natural minor **(nat. min.)**.

1. _____ 2. _____ 3. _____ 4. _____ 5. _____ 6. _____